PLAYBOOK

for

PARENTS

Praying Powerful Prayers over Your Athlete

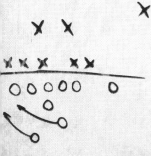

Jeff and Rachel Lovingood

Hi Friend—

Congratulations! Your son or daughter (or athlete you care about) is reaching his or her dream of playing sports at the next level. Do you remember as parents of young athletes how we would spend much of our time driving them to practice, fixing snacks, talking through the game and coaching them up? As they got older our roles changed in their lives but we were still very involved even if much of it happened after practice or after the games. Then when they make it to the next level—to college ball or professional ball, suddenly we have nothing familiar to do. Our input into their athletics is vastly different and we can find ourselves wondering what we are supposed to do now. Now that they've achieved some of their goals, what can we do?

Now is the time when we need to focus on the most important thing we can do as a parent of an athlete at the next level. Now is when we should spend our time involved in the most powerful tool at our disposal that can strengthen our athletes beyond our imaginations—we can pray.

Where they used to rely on us now they have coaches, trainers, GA's and nutritionists. Instead of doing nothing, now is the time to do the best thing—pray powerful prayers.

This Playbook for Parents offers you organized prayers that are straight from Scripture and focuses on different topics that are applicable to athletes. Each day lists the Scripture verse for that day and then a written out prayer using the verse. You can pray them in order or find the topic that your athlete has most need of that day. The prayers are open ended so that you can use them to get started and then continue your conversation with the Lord about anything else. The prayers are written for male athletes but feel free to adjust that as you pray for your female athletes too.

When we pray we put ourselves and the one we pray for into the hands of Almighty God and trust that He can make a difference. It's the best play in the book for us as parents or people who care about our athletes and it is a win every time.

Thank you for caring about your athlete enough to do the best thing for him or her—

Jeff and Rachel Lovingood

TABLE OF CONTENTS

FOR ADDITIONAL SUPPORT
AND ENCOURAGEMENT, FOLLOW
@PLAYBOOK4PRNTS ON
SOCIAL MEDIA.

USE @PLAYBOOK4PRNTS TO SHARE PRAYER
REQUESTS AND
CELEBRATE ANSWERED PRAYERS.

"He said to them: "It is not for you to know the times or dates the Father has set by his own authority. But you will receive power when the Holy Spirit comes on you; and you will be my witnesses in Jerusalem, and in all Judea and Samaria, and to the ends of the earth."

ACTS 1:7-8

Almighty God,

Just as you said that we don't have to know the date or the time because you have set those by your authority-thank you for the promise of power through the Holy Spirit. I pray that you will pour out your Spirit on _____ and let him experience your power so that he can be your witness in Jerusalem, Judea and Samaria and to the ends of the earth. Father with the world of technology we live in and the focus on athletics I know that you can use _____ as a witness to the very ends of the earth and I pray that you will remind him of the privilege to be used by you and the responsibility he has to represent you well not on his own strength but by the power of the Holy Spirit...

* **P O W E R** *

"Do not be anxious about anything, but in everything, by prayer and petition, with thanksgiving, present your requests to God. And the peace of God, which transcends all understanding, will guard your hearts and your minds in Christ Jesus."

PHILIPPIANS 4:6-7

God,

This is an anxious world we live in and what _____ is facing regularly can easily add to worry and stress. Father help ____ to be anxious for nothing but Lord, to pray and offer his requests to you. Let him be thankful in all things as he turns to you with his stresses and questions. Then Lord please guard _____'s heart and mind with your peace that passes understanding. Only through your power and presence can peace be possible, so show yourself to _____ in a very real way...

* P E A C E *

"See to it, brothers, that none of you has a sinful, unbelieving heart that turns away from the living God. But encourage one another daily, as long as it is called Today, so that none of you may be hardened by sin's deceitfulness. We have come to share in Christ if we hold firmly till the end the confidence we had at first. As has just been said: "Today, if you hear his voice, do not harden your hearts as you did in the rebellion."

HEBREWS 3:12-15

Lord,

Thank you that you want ____ to hear from you and to walk
in your way. Keep ____ from having a sinful,
unbelieving heart that could turn him away from you. Let
_____ instead encourage those around him and be
encouraged so that he may never be hardened by sin's
deceitfulness. Strengthen _____'s confidence in you so
that he can hold firmly to it and to be careful that he
doesn't let his heart grow hardened. Speak to _____ and let
him be listening to your voice today...

* **EARS TO HEAR** *

"He will wipe every tear from their eyes. There will be no more death or mourning or crying or pain, for the old order of things has passed away."

REVELATION 21:4

Father,

You know how hard it can be to deal with all that athletes face on and off the field. Whether it is physical or emotional pain and suffering, let ___ always recognize that you alone have the power to wipe away every tear from his eyes. Thank you that death shall be no more neither will there be mourning, nor crying nor pain anymore because the former things will have passed away. Help _____ endure the pain of today because he knows it will not last and his trust and faith are securely in you. Give him faith to look to the future and trust your plans for him...

"Finally, be strong in the Lord and in his mighty power. Put on the full armor of God so that you can take your stand against the devil's schemes. For our struggle is not against flesh and blood, but against the rulers, against the authorities, against the powers of this dark world and against the spiritual forces of evil in the heavenly realms"

EPHESIANS 6:10-12

Lord Jesus,

Let _____ be strong in you and in your mighty power. Clothe him in your armor so that he can stand against the schemes of the devil. Let him remember that his struggle is not against flesh and blood even when it seems like it is, but against rulers, authorities, powers and spiritual forces in this dark world-- so be his strength and fight for him when the enemy tries to steal his witness and distract him from doing your will. May your plans for ____ never be disrupted...

* S T R E N G T H *

"Not only so, but we also rejoice in our sufferings, because we know that suffering produces perseverance; perseverance, character; and character, hope. And hope does not disappoint us, because God has poured out his love into our hearts by the Holy Spirit, whom he has given us."

ROMANS 5:3-5

Father,

You know how things can go badly in athletics and as a
    player who has pressure to perform at a high level,
        suffering is pretty much inevitable at some point.
        Whether _____ suffers from unjust things, from
physical pain or injuries or anything else, let him learn
to rejoice in his sufferings because you can cause them
to produce perseverance then character and then hope.
Thank you that hope does not disappoint and use it in
_____'s life as you pour out your love into his heart by the
Holy Spirit. Please do not let ___ get discouraged but keep
him focused on the good you can produce from everything
            in his life whether good or bad...

* S U F F E R I N G *

"Because of the LORD's great love we are not consumed, for his compassions never fail. They are new every morning; great is your faithfulness. I say to myself, "The LORD is my portion; therefore I will wait for him." The LORD is good to those whose hope is in him, to the one who seeks him."

LAMENTATIONS 3:22-25

Lord,

Thank you that your love never ceases that your mercies never come to an end. No matter what happened yesterday—your mercies are new every day and great is your faithfulness. Let these truths be an encouragement and a source of strength for _____ today. Let his soul recognize that you are his portion and let _____ find his hope in you because you are good to those who wait for you and to the soul who seeks you. Give _____ the desire to seek after you in all he does...

"Finally, brothers, we instructed you how to live in order to please God, as in fact you are living. Now we ask you and urge you in the Lord Jesus to do this more and more. For you know what instructions we gave you by the authority of the Lord Jesus. It is God's will that you should be sanctified: that you should avoid sexual immorality; that each of you should learn to control his own body in a way that is holy and honorable"

1 THESSALONIANS 4:1-4

Lord God,

Let _____ choose to walk in your way and to please you
with his life. Give him a desire to know your
instructions and to follow them so that he can fulfill your
will and be sanctified. Let _____ abstain from
sexual immorality as he controls his body in holiness and
honor so that his walk is pleasing and honoring to you and
that you are glorified in his life. Let the way that _____
chooses to live be a positive influence on those he is around
and let his life bear witness to your grace and mercy...

* SELF CONTROL *

"The most important one," answered Jesus, "is this: 'Hear, O Israel, the Lord our God, the Lord is one. Love the Lord your God with all your heart and with all your soul and with all your mind and with all your strength.'"

MARK 12:29-30

Lord Jesus,

You made it very clear what is important to you. In the world that throws so many things at _____ that are all competing for a place of importance, help him to remember you are the Lord our God. Help _____ to love you with all his heart, soul, mind and strength so that his thoughts, desires, words and actions are all reflections of his relationship with you. Draw him closer to you today...

* F A I T H *

"But I trust in you, O LORD; I say, "You are my God." My times are in your hands; deliver me from my enemies and from those who pursue me. Let your face shine on your servant; save me in your unfailing love."

PSALM 31:14-16

Lord God,

You alone are worthy of trust. Let the truth of that be evident to _____ today. Let him say "You are my God" as he trusts in you. Help _____ recognize that his days are in your hands so that you alone should be in control of those days. Deliver _____ from his enemies and those who pursue him with evil intent. Let your face shine on your servant _____ and save him in your unfailing love...

* **T R U S T** *

"And God is able to make every grace overflow to you, so that in every way, always having everything you need, you may excel in every good work."

2 Corinthians 9:8 (HCSB)

Father God,

Thank you that you are able to make every grace overflow to _____ so that in every way he will always have everything he needs. Let _____ live by faith in you so that he excels in every good work whether it is on the field, in the class or anywhere else he goes. Let ____ remember that anything he does should be done with excellence because it is a testimony to you – the God he serves. Bless his efforts and use him for your glory...

* **E X C E L** *

"Praise be to the God and Father of our Lord Jesus Christ, the Father of compassion and the God of all comfort, who comforts us in all our troubles, so that we can comfort those in any trouble with the comfort we ourselves have received from God. For just as the sufferings of Christ flow over into our lives, so also through Christ our comfort overflows. If we are distressed, it is for your comfort and salvation; if we are comforted, it is for your comfort, which produces in you patient endurance of the same sufferings we suffer. And our hope for you is firm, because we know that just as you share in our sufferings, so also you share in our comfort."

2 CORINTHIANS 1:3-7

O god,

I praise you Lord the Father of compassion and the god of all comfort. Please comfort _____ in all his troubles so that he can comfort others with troubles with what he has received from you. Let the comfort of Christ that flows over _____ cause comfort to overflow from _____. When he is distressed let _____ find comfort in you and let the troubles he faces regularly produce patient endurance and let him hold firm to his hope in you because you have shared in his sufferings as well as his comfort...

* S U F F E R I N G *

"Command and teach these things. Let no one despise your youth; instead, you should be an example to the believers in speech, in conduct, in love, in faith, in purity. Pay close attention to your life and your teaching; persevere in these things, for by doing this you will save both yourself and your hearers."

1 TIMOTHY 4:11-12, 16 (HCSB)

Lord,

Thank you that you use us regardless of age or position in life. Although ____ may not be the most senior member on the team let him take seriously your charge to be an example for all. Let _____ be a good example in speech, conduct, love, faith and purity. Remind him to pay close attention to his life and your teaching as he perseveres in his faith. Thank you that you can use his life to save and encourage others. Give him opportunities to represent you as you choose to expand his horizons...

"Therefore, since we have been justified through faith, we have peace with God through our Lord Jesus Christ, through whom we have gained access by faith into this grace in which we now stand. And we rejoice in the hope of the glory of God."

ROMANS 5:1-2

God,

Thank you that _____ has been justified by faith and that means he can have peace with you through our Lord Jesus Christ and that he has access into your grace by faith. There are many things in _____'s life that have nothing to do with peace so please plant this truth in his heart firmly so that peace becomes the norm for him and don't let him settle for stress over peace. Let _____ rejoice in the hope of the glory of God. Speak truth and peace into his heart and life today...

* **P E A C E** *

"Do not rejoice over me, my enemy! Though I have fallen, I will stand up; though I sit in darkness, the LORD will be my light."

MICAH 7:8 (HCSB)

Father,

There are enemies all around that are seeking to defeat _____ and bring him down. Do not let them rejoice over _____ because though he might fall Lord you can make him stand up and though it might seem dark—you Lord are the light. Be the light to _____ when things seem darkest and let him trust in your Truth and your light. Be the lifter of his head and the strength he needs today...

"Though I walk in the
midst of trouble, you preserve my life;
you stretch out your hand against the
anger of my foes, with your right hand
you save me."

Psalm 138:7

Lord,

Thank you that you want ____ to hear from you and to walk in your way. Keep ____ from having a sinful, unbelieving heart that could turn him away from you. Let _____ instead encourage those around him and be encouraged so that he may never be hardened by sin's deceitfulness. Strengthen _____'s confidence in you so that he can hold firmly to it and to be careful that he doesn't let his heart grow hardened. Speak to _____ and let him be listening to your voice today...

"So do not fear, for I am with you; do not be dismayed, for I am your God. I will strengthen you and help you; I will uphold you with my righteous right hand. "All who rage against you will surely be ashamed and disgraced; those who oppose you will be as nothing and perish. Though you search for your enemies, you will not find them. Those who wage war against you will be as nothing at all. For I am the LORD, your God, who takes hold of your right hand and says to you, Do not fear; I will help you."

ISAIAH 41:10-13

O god,

Keep ____ from fear because he knows you are with him. Do not let him be dismayed for you are his god and you will strengthen _____ and help him. Uphold him with your righteous right hand. Thank you that all who rage against ____ will surely be ashamed and disgraced and that those who oppose him will be nothing and perish. Let ____ not even be able to find his enemies and let those who wage war against him be as nothing at all because you are the Lord, the god who takes hold of _____'s right hand. Let _____ never fear for you will help him...

* S T R E N G T H *

"And lead us not into temptation, but deliver us from the evil one."

Matthew 6:13

18

Lord God,

There are so many temptations that come against _____ on a regular basis. Please give him wisdom and discernment as you lead him AWAY from temptation and not into it. Please use your mighty power to deliver _____ from the evil one and protect him as only you can. Let ____ trust in you and give him wisdom to see the way out of bad situations...

* TEMPTATION *

"This is what the LORD says to you: 'Do not be afraid or discouraged because of this vast army. For the battle is not yours, but God's. You will not have to fight this battle. Take up your positions; stand firm and see the deliverance the LORD will give you, O Judah and Jerusalem. Do not be afraid; do not be discouraged. Go out to face them tomorrow, and the LORD will be with you."

2 CHRONICLES 20:15, 17

19

Almighty God,

Thank you that _____ need never be discouraged or afraid no matter who or what is coming against him. Let _____ know and believe that the battle is not his to fight alone but it is yours god. Thank you that he does not have to fight the battle on his strength but let him stand firm and see your deliverance. Keep him from fear and discouragement in the face of battle because he knows you are with him. Fill him with your power and strength because you love him and have great plans for his life...

* STRENGTH *

"Therefore, since we are surrounded by so great a cloud of witnesses, let us also lay aside every weight, and sin which clings so closely, and let us run with endurance the race that is set before us, looking to Jesus, the founder and perfecter of our faith, who for the joy that was set before him endured the cross, despising the shame, and is seated at the right hand of the throne of God."

HEBREWS 12:1-2 (ESV)

20

Lord Jesus,

Thank you that you have wisdom for every situation.

Remind ____ that there are always witnesses watching him and let that be motivation for him to keep his life honoring to you. Help him lay aside the things that are weighing him down and the sin that easily entangles so that he can run with endurance the race you've set before him. Jesus, let ___ keep his eyes on you the founder and perfecter of his faith because you Jesus endured so much more than any human can comprehend and then took your place beside the throne of God. Let _____ be encouraged by remembering that you can relate to pressure and watching eyes and let him trust you to be his strength in all things...

＊ E N D U R A N C E ＊

"For it is by grace you have been saved, through faith--and this not from yourselves, it is the gift of God-- not by works, so that no one can boast. For we are God's workmanship, created in Christ Jesus to do good works, which God prepared in advance for us to do."

EPHESIANS 2:8-10

21

Lord God,

Thank you that you have saved _____ through faith and it's not anything he ever did or could do. Thank you for the gift of salvation. Let _____ firmly recognize that he is your workmanship created in Christ Jesus to do good works that you prepared in advance for him to do. Right now you have _____ playing on his team and you have great plans for how you want to use him. Let him be available to all that you are planning to use him for and be glorified in his life. Help him stand firm on who he knows you created him to be and not listen to any untruths that others might use to undermine him and destroy his confidence....

* C O N F I D E N C E *

"So then, banish anxiety from your heart and cast off the troubles of your body, for youth and vigor are meaningless."

ECCLESIASTES 11:10

22

Oh god,

How stressful the world of athletics can be. Thank you that you alone can banish anxiety from _____'s heart and cast any troubles off his body so that he can be full of youth and vigor again. Remove the pain and the worry that accompanies stress and physical troubles and help _____ to trust in your great plan. Thank you that you are bigger and stronger than anything that ____ has to deal with today. Show yourself to be real to him today...

"Now to him who is able to keep you from stumbling and to present you blameless before the presence of his glory with great joy, to the only God, our Savior, through Jesus Christ our Lord, be glory, majesty, dominion, and authority, before all time and now and forever. Amen."

JUDE 1:24-25 (ESV)

23

Lord,

What a blessing it is to know that you can keep us from stumbling. Please keep _____ on firm footing in the culture he faces that tries to trip him up constantly. Thank you that you are the firm foundation he needs to stand on and thank you that you can keep him blameless before you. I praise you God for all your glory, majesty, dominion, and authority and I ask that you reveal those aspects of your character to _____ in a real way so that his faith in you grows and so he can know you better...

* **STAND FIRM** *

"To you, O LORD, I lift up my soul; in you I trust, O my God. Do not let me be put to shame, nor let my enemies triumph over me."

PSALM 25:1-2

"Those who know your name will trust in you, for you, LORD, have never forsaken those who seek you."

PSALM 9:10

24

O Lord,

There are many enemies that come against _____. People who have agendas and who don't necessarily want your best for him. Continually let _____ trust in you. Lift up his soul. Do not let him be put to shame or let his enemies triumph over him. Let _____ know you more each day so that he will trust in you more each day. Thank you that you are all powerful, worthy of trust and that you will never forsake _____. Let these truths comfort him today...

* T R U S T *

"Be strong and courageous, because you will lead these people to inherit the land I swore to their forefathers to give them. Be strong and very courageous. Be careful to obey all the law my servant Moses gave you; do not turn from it to the right or to the left, that you may be successful wherever you go."

JOSHUA 1:6-8

25

Almighty God,

Be with _____. Help him to be strong and courageous because you are with him and you have plans for his life.

In the face of people and circumstances that challenge his strength, let him always be strong and very courageous. Keep _____ focused on your Word so that he will obey it and not turn from it to the right or the left. Thank you that your Word has everything _____ needs to be successful wherever he goes as long as he obeys it. Help him to see the value of living by your Word and not by the ways of the world...

"My soul finds rest in God alone; my salvation comes from him. He alone is my rock and my salvation; he is my fortress, I will never be shaken."

PSALM 62:1-2

26

Father God,

With pressure coming on him from all sides, let _____ find rest in you God. Thank you that his salvation comes from you and not from his works. God prove yourself to be _____'s rock and salvation. Thank you for being his fortress so that he will never be shaken. Strengthen _____'s confidence because of who you are. Give him peace and rest today as he faces down pressure of all kinds...

* P R E S S U R E *

" Beloved, I pray that all may go well with you and that you may be in good health, as it goes well with your soul. "

3 JOHN 1:2 (ESV)

27

Lord Jesus,

Thank you that you see and know everything about us and that nothing escapes your gaze. During this intense season that _____ is facing would you keep him in good health physically? Thank you that you care about his physical and his spiritual side as well as his soul. So would you also protect his soul Lord? Put a hedge of protection around ____ in every way and watch over him as only you can and keep him whole and healthy in every area of his life...

* H E A L T H *

"To man belong the plans of the heart, but from the LORD comes the reply of the tongue. All a man's ways seem innocent to him, but motives are weighed by the LORD. Commit to the LORD whatever you do, and your plans will succeed."

PROVERBS 16:1-3

28

Father,

It's so cool that you know everything about us even to the motives of our hearts and what is behind our plans. As _____ makes plans both immediate and long term would you speak wisdom to him? Where his motives may be off, guide ____ in the way he should go and make his heart sensitive to your Holy Spirit. Help _____ commit all he does to you recognizing that it's the only way his plans will succeed. Keep him focused on your plans and your ways. Thank you that you care about everything and you have the best plans for _____...

COMMITMENT

"Above all else, guard your heart, for it is the wellspring of life. Put away perversity from your mouth; keep corrupt talk far from your lips. Let your eyes look straight ahead, fix your gaze directly before you. Make level paths for your feet and take only ways that are firm. Do not swerve to the right or the left; keep your foot from evil."

PROVERBS 4:23-26

29

Lord Jesus,

Above all else, help _____ to guard his heart for it is the wellspring of life. Let him put away perversity from his mouth and keep corrupt talk from his lips. Keep _____ 's eyes looking straight ahead and fix his gaze on you. Make level paths for his feet and let _____ only take ways that are firm. Give him focus to stay straight ahead not to the right or left and keep his foot from evil. Please give _____ extreme clarity about the choices he makes and the directions he goes...

"Trust in the LORD with all your heart and lean not on your own understanding; in all your ways acknowledge him, and he will make your paths straight. Do not be wise in your own eyes; fear the LORD and shun evil. This will bring health to your body and nourishment to your bones."

PROVERBS 3:5-8

30

Lord,

Today help ____ to trust in you with all his heart and lean not on his own understanding. Also let ____ acknowledge you in all his ways and then thank you that you will make his path straight. Keep _____ from becoming wise in his own eyes and let him fear you as he shuns evil. God please bring health to _____ body and nourishment to his bones. Thank you that your Word is true and you keep your promises. Let ____'s life be a testimony to you and a witness to others...

"Do you not know? Have you not heard? The LORD is the everlasting God, the Creator of the ends of the earth. He will not grow tired or weary, and his understanding no one can fathom. He gives strength to the weary and increases the power of the weak. Even youths grow tired and weary, and young men stumble and fall; but those who hope in the LORD will renew their strength. They will soar on wings like eagles; they will run and not grow weary, they will walk and not be faint."

ISAIAH 40:28-31

31

God,

I know that _____ gets so tired and weary. Remind him that you are the everlasting God, the Creator of the ends of the earth and you never grow tired or weary and your understanding is beyond comprehension. Thank you that you give strength to the weary and increase the power of the weak. Even when _____ grows tired or weary or even stumbles and falls, let _____ hope in you so that you can renew his strength. Let him soar on wings like eagles. Let him run and not grow weary. Let him walk and not faint all because _____ trusts and hopes in you...

* **W E A R Y** *

"But he said to me, "My grace is sufficient for you, for my power is made perfect in weakness." Therefore I will boast all the more gladly about my weaknesses, so that Christ's power may rest on me. That is why, for Christ's sake, I delight in weaknesses, in insults, in hardships, in persecutions, in difficulties. For when I am weak, then I am strong."

2 CORINTHIANS 12:9-10

32

O God,

Thank you that your grace is sufficient for _____ and your power is made perfect in weakness. Although he lives in a world that pushes him to be perfect let ____ understand that recognizing his weaknesses gives him an opportunity to tap into more of your power. Help _____ see how facing weakness, insults, hardships, persecutions and difficulties can be moments when he can experience even more of your power because when he recognizes his own limited strength then he will also recognize your unbelievable power. Show yourself strong on behalf of _____ and let him trust in you today...

* **P O W E R** *

"Therefore, brothers, since we have confidence to enter the Most Holy Place by the blood of Jesus, by a new and living way opened for us through the curtain, that is, his body, Let us hold unswervingly to the hope we profess, for he who promised is faithful."

HEBREWS 10:19-20, 23

33

Father god,

Thank you for the confidence that you give through the blood of Jesus that allows ____ into your presence. Thank you Jesus for your sacrifice on the cross that made the way and let ____ hold unswervingly to the hope he professes because you are faithful. Please continue to show yourself faithful to _____ and draw him into your presence so that his confidence in you will grow...

* C O N S I S T E N T *

"In the same way, count yourselves dead to sin but alive to God in Christ Jesus. Therefore do not let sin reign in your mortal body so that you obey its evil desires. Do not offer the parts of your body to sin, as instruments of wickedness, but rather offer yourselves to God, as those who have been brought from death to life; and offer the parts of your body to him as instruments of righteousness. For sin shall not be your master, because you are not under law, but under grace."

ROMANS 6:11-14

34

Dear Lord,

Let _____ count himself dead to sin but alive to you Lord in Christ Jesus. Don't let sin reign in _____'s body so that he obeys its evil desires. Keep _____ from offering any part of his body to sin as an instrument of wickedness but rather let _____ offer himself to you God as one who has been brought from death to life and offer his body as an instrument of righteousness. Please do NOT let sin be _____'s master because he is not under the law but under grace and let him live in that freedom in a way that honors you...

"My flesh and my heart may fail, but God is the strength of my heart and my portion forever."

PSALM 73:26

35

Lord,

Things won't always happen the way he wants or expects them to so when things don't go perfectly and when _____ feels down or discouraged remind him that You, Lord are the strength of his heart and his portion forever. Although he may be tempted to doubt or look elsewhere for strength, God, show him that true strength comes from you and you will never let him down...

* **F A I L U R E** *

"No, in all these things we are more than conquerors through him who loved us. For I am convinced that neither death nor life, neither angels nor demons, neither the present nor the future, nor any powers, neither height nor depth, nor anything else in all creation, will be able to separate us from the love of God that is in Christ Jesus our Lord."

ROMANS 8:37-38

36

Lord god,

Thank you that in all things _____ is more than a conqueror through you. Thank you that neither death nor life, neither angels nor demons, neither the present nor the future, nor any powers, neither height nor depth, nor anything else in all creation will be able to separate ____ from your love, O god, that is in Christ Jesus our Lord. When _____ faces those who are trying to beat him or wear him down, let him always

remember this and live like a conqueror because in you he is...

"From the ends of the earth I call to you, I call as my heart grows faint; lead me to the rock that is higher than I. For you have been my refuge, a strong tower against the foe. I long to dwell in your tent forever and take refuge in the shelter of your wings."

PSALM 61:2-4

37

O Lord,

Thank you for being there when _____ calls out to you. If and when his heart may grow faint lead him to turn to you and lead him to the rock that is higher than he is. Thank you for being his refuge and strong tower against his foes. Give him peace and rest in your presence. Help ____ to focus on you and trust in you instead of giving any attention to those who come against him...

* R E S T *

"For though we live in the world, we do not wage war as the world does. The weapons we fight with are not the weapons of the world. On the contrary, they have divine power to demolish strongholds. We demolish arguments and every pretension that sets itself up against the knowledge of God, and we take captive every thought to make it obedient to Christ."

2 Corinthians 10:3-5

38

Lord God,

Although he is living in this world with all kinds of opposition, thank you that ____ as a believer does not wage war like the world does. Let _____ remember that the weapons we fight with are not the weapons of the world but our weapons have divine power to demolish strongholds. Father demolish all arguments and every pretension that sets itself up against the knowledge of God and let _____ take captive every thought to make it obedient to Christ Jesus. Let him believe the Truth over the lies and the false teachings he may encounter. Let ___ fight his battles in your power and strength today...

"And pray in the Spirit on all occasions with all kinds of prayers and requests. With this in mind, be alert and always keep on praying for all the saints."

EPHESIANS 6:18

39

O Lord,

When the day to day pressures don't let up. When ____ feels tired or worn out would you remind him that you are there? Would you draw him to seek you and pray to you in all situations and circumstances? Thank you that there is nothing _____ can't pray about. Help him to be alert to keep on praying at all times for his teammates and coaches as well as himself...

PERSEVERANCE

"How can a young man keep his way pure? By guarding it according to your word. With my whole heart I seek you; let me not wander from your commandments! I have stored up your word in my heart, that I might not sin against you."

Psalm 119:9-11 (ESV)

40

Father God,

It is not easy in this world for a young man to keep his way pure so help ____ to do that by guarding his life according to your Word. With his whole heart let _____ seek after you and not wander from your commandments. Store up your Word in his heart that he might not sin against you. When _____ is facing a major choice or temptation, bring your Word to his mind and protect, guide and direct him...

"He will wipe every tear from their eyes. There will be no more death or mourning or crying or pain, for the old order of things has passed away."

REVELATION 21:4

41

Lord Jesus,

Please help ____ remain steadfast under trials that will come his way. Bless him for standing firm and let him receive the crown of life you have promised to those who love you. Don't let ____ ever say or believe that he is being tempted by you because you cannot be tempted with evil nor do you tempt anyone, but let ____ recognize that when he is tempted that he is being lured and enticed by his own desire and let him see how dangerous that desire can be as it leads from desire to sin that leads to broken fellowship with you. Keep ____ close to you and help him to see sin and temptation for what they really are and to resist the temptations by your power at work in him...

* **P A I N** *

"Blessed is the man who perseveres under trial, because when he has stood the test, he will receive the crown of life that God has promised to those who love him. When tempted, no one should say, "God is tempting me." For God cannot be tempted by evil, nor does he tempt anyone; but each one is tempted when, by his own evil desire, he is dragged away and enticed. Then, after desire has conceived, it gives birth to sin; and sin, when it is full-grown, gives birth to death."

James 1:12-15

42

Lord Jesus,

Please help ____ remain steadfast under

trials that will come his way. Bless him for standing firm

and let him receive the crown of life you have promised to

those who love you. Don't let ____ ever say or believe that

he is being tempted by you because you cannot be tempted

with evil nor do you tempt anyone, but let ____ recognize

that when he is tempted that he is being lured and

enticed by his own desire and let him see how dangerous

that desire can be as it leads from desire to sin that

leads to broken fellowship with you. Keep ____ close to you

and help him to see sin and temptation for what they

really are and to resist the temptations by your power at

work in him...

* S T R E N G T H *

"Let us draw near to God with a sincere heart in full assurance of faith, having our hearts sprinkled to cleanse us from a guilty conscience and having our bodies washed with pure water. Let us hold unswervingly to the hope we profess, for he who promised is faithful. And let us consider how we may spur one another on toward love and good deeds. Let us not give up meeting together, as some are in the habit of doing, but let us encourage one another--and all the more as you see the Day approaching."

HEBREWS 10:22-25

43

Lord Jesus,

Would you draw _____ to you with a true heart in full assurance of faith even under circumstances that tend to create doubt? Father sprinkle his heart clean from any evil conscience and cleanse him with pure water. Let ____ always hold fast to his confession of hope without wavering because you promised and you are faithful. Let _____ consider how to stir up others to good works and not to withdraw but to continue gathering with others for encouragement. Bring people into _____'s circle of influence who will be encouragers to him and also that he can encourage. As so many look to tear down, Father, show _____ how to build up and be used by you...

* **F A I T H** *

"Finally, be strong in the Lord and in the strength of his might. Put on the whole armor of God, that you may be able to stand against the schemes of the devil. For we do not wrestle against flesh and blood, but against the rulers, against the authorities, against the cosmic powers over this present darkness, against the spiritual forces of evil in the heavenly places. Therefore take up the whole armor of God, that you may be able to withstand in the evil day, and having done all, to stand firm."

Ephesians 6:10-13 (ESV)

44

Lord Jesus,

Help _____ to be strong in you and in your mighty strength.
Clothe him with your armor so that he can stand firm
against the schemes of the devil. Although _____ does
battle on the field against real people, Father the true
battle is fought against spiritual forces of evil in heavenly
places—therefore God, do not let _____ go out unprepared
for the battle. Remind him that you are on his side and
that when he clothes himself in your armor that he will
be able to withstand in the day of evil and after all is said
and done to stand firm! Thank you Lord that you desire
_____ to be victorious in you...

* P R O T E C T I O N *

"Finally, all of you, live in harmony with one another; be sympathetic, love as brothers, be compassionate and humble. Do not repay evil with evil or insult with insult, but with blessing, because to this you were called so that you may inherit a blessing. For, "Whoever would love life and see good days must keep his tongue from evil and his lips from deceitful speech. He must turn from evil and do good; he must seek peace and pursue it. For the eyes of the Lord are on the righteous and his ears are attentive to their prayer, but the face of the Lord is against those who do evil."

1 PETER 3:8-12

45

Lord,

You know how crazy life on a team can be and yet you tell us to have unity. Help _____ to have unity of mind, sympathy, brotherly love, a tender heart and a humble mind especially as he is part of the team. Do not let _____ repay evil with evil but to bless others and then Lord please bless him. Keep _____'s tongue from evil and his lips from speaking deceit, let him turn away from evil and do good, let him seek peace and pursue it. Thank you that your eyes are on the righteous and your ears are open to their prayer-let that be _____. See him and hear him and keep him in your will...

* **T E A M** *

"May he give you the desire of your heart and make all your plans succeed. We will shout for joy when you are victorious and will lift up our banners in the name of our God. May the LORD grant all your requests."

Psalm 20:4-5

46

O god,

Thank you that you bless those who seek after you. Would you direct _____'s heart toward you so that his desires are your desires and his plans can succeed? Lord we will shout for joy when _____ is victorious and give you the praise and glory. Keep ____ focused on you and your ways so that you can bless him and let him recognize that all blessings come from you. I love you...

* V I C T O R Y *

"Now to Him who is able to do exceedingly abundantly above all that we ask or think, according to the power that works in us, to Him be glory in the church by Christ Jesus to all generations, forever and ever. Amen."

EPHESIANS 3:20-21 (NKJV)

47

Lord God,

You alone are worthy of praise and you alone have the power to do incredibly great and mighty things. Thank you that you are the Lord who is able to do exceedingly abundantly more that we can ask or imagine according to your power at work in us. Lord exert your power in _____'s life. Let him experience the unbelievable and the impossible because of your power at work in him. I give you all the glory now and forever because you deserve it...

EXPECTATIONS

"Be self-controlled and alert. Your enemy the devil prowls around like a roaring lion looking for someone to devour. Resist him, standing firm in the faith, because you know that your brothers throughout the world are undergoing the same kind of sufferings. And the God of all grace, who called you to his eternal glory in Christ, after you have suffered a little while, will himself restore you and make you strong, firm and steadfast."

1 PETER 5:8-11

48

Lord Jesus,

Please be with _____ and help him be self controlled and alert in the crazy world he lives in. Protect him from the enemy that is prowling around looking to devour him. Give _____ strength to resist the devil and stand firm in his faith as he realizes that other believers are struggling in the same ways around the world. Thank you that you-the God of all grace-called _____to be yours. Please make _____strong, firm and steadfast in you and by your power...

"Therefore, there is now no condemnation for those who are in Christ Jesus, because through Christ Jesus the law of the Spirit of life set me free from the law of sin and death."

ROMANS 8:1-2

49

Lord Jesus,

In the world of athletics it is so easy for players to get down on themselves for all kinds of reasons. Please remind ＿＿＿＿＿ that there is no condemnation for those who are in Christ Jesus because he has been set free through you when you set him free from the law of sin and death. Be the lifter of his head and let him always know and believe that he is your loved child and you are his biggest fan...

"Have nothing to do with irreverent, silly myths. Rather train yourself for godliness; for while bodily training is of some value, godliness is of value in every way, as it holds promise for the present life and also for the life to come. The saying is trustworthy and deserving of full acceptance. For to this end we toil and strive, because we have our hope set on the living God, who is the Savior of all people, especially of those who believe."

1 TIMOTHY 4:7-10 (ESV)

50

Father,

In the midst of all the physical and mental training that ----- is going through, reinforce to him of the value of spiritual training. Let ----- never overlook the importance of developing himself spiritually while he is developing himself physically because of the great value that spiritual training has both in this life and the one to come. Keep his hope set on you the living God who is Savior of all people. Give ----- a hunger to know you and live for you...

DISCIPLINE

"Now I know that the LORD saves his anointed; he answers him from his holy heaven with the saving power of his right hand. Some trust in chariots and some in horses, but we trust in the name of the LORD our God. They are brought to their knees and fall, but we rise up and stand firm."

PSALM 20:6-8

51

Lord God,

You are worthy of complete trust and faith. In this culture that tells us to trust in self, help _____ to remember that you are the one who saves the anointed and that you will answer him from heaven with the saving power of your right hand. Keep _____ from placing his trust in anything other than you because those things will fail at some point but you never will. Thank you that when he trusts in you that you will cause _____ to rise up and stand firm...

* **T R U S T** *

"Commit your way to the LORD; trust in him and he will do this: He will make your righteousness shine like the dawn, the justice of your cause like the noonday sun. Be still before the LORD and wait patiently for him; do not fret when men succeed in their ways, when they carry out their wicked schemes. Refrain from anger and turn from wrath; do not fret-- it leads only to evil."

Psalm 37:5-8

52

Lord Jesus,

Thank you that you promise to do what only you can do when ____ commits his way to you and trusts in you. Help ____ to be still before you and to wait patiently for you. Help him resist the urge to fret when men succeed in their ways as they carry out their evil schemes. Keep ____ from anger and let him turn from wrath without being anxious...

* C O M M I T *

"Fear not, for I have redeemed you; I have summoned you by name; you are mine. When you pass through the waters, I will be with you; and when you pass through the rivers, they will not sweep over you. When you walk through the fire, you will not be burned; the flames will not set you ablaze. For I am the LORD, your God, the Holy One of Israel, your Savior."

ISAIAH 43:1-3

53

O Lord,

When fear tries to creep into _____'s life, don't let it. Help ____ to fear NOT because you have redeemed him and he is yours. Make it clear to ____ that you will be with him no matter where he goes and what he does. Thank you that when he passes through the waters or the rivers that he will not be swept away. When ____ walks through the fire you will not let him be burned or set ablaze because you are the Lord, the Holy One of Israel—the Savior. Thank you for watching over _____ and being a constant presence in his life...

* **F E A R** *

"Therefore, I urge you, brothers, in view of God's mercy, to offer your bodies as living sacrifices, holy and pleasing to God--this is your spiritual act of worship. Do not conform any longer to the pattern of this world, but be transformed by the renewing of your mind. Then you will be able to test and approve what God's will is--his good, pleasing and perfect will."

ROMANS 12:1-2

54

O god,

   Today let _____ choose to present his body as a living
   sacrifice, holy acceptable to you as his spiritual act of
worship. Help him see the value in offering his body to be
used by you and all the implications that come with that.
Do not let _____ be conformed to this world but transform
him by the renewing of his mind that he may test and
   know what your good, acceptable and perfect will is...

"Praise be to the Lord, to God our Savior, who daily bears our burdens. Selah Our God is a God who saves; from the Sovereign LORD comes escape from death. Surely God will crush the heads of his enemies, the hairy crowns of those who go on in their sins."

PSALM 68:19-21

55

Lord God,

Thank you that you are Savior and that you bear our
burdens so we don't have to carry them alone. There are
so many things that weigh _____ down and become heavy
burdens for him to carry-be there for _____. Lift those
burdens from his shoulders and remind him that you are
the God who saves and that you alone have the power
to crush the heads of the Enemy who comes after him.
Bless _____ today and let him walk secure in knowing
that you are in control and that he is not alone in what he
is going through. Thank you for having his back...

* **DAILY BURDENS** *

"He who walks with the wise grows wise,
but a companion of fools suffers harm."

PROVERBS 13:20

56

Father God,

Give _____ wisdom and discernment as he chooses people to spend time with. Guard his mind and help him make wise choices about who he allows into his inner circle and let them be people that he can trust to make him wise. Keep ___ from fools as companions and thus keep him from harm that comes from spending time with those who make foolish choices. Thank you for warning ____ about who he befriends and use him to be a friend that makes others more wise. Let _____ bring those around him up to a higher level and influence them for your good and your glory...

* F R I E N D S *

"Brothers, if someone is caught in a sin, you who are spiritual should restore him gently. But watch yourself, or you also may be tempted. Carry each other's burdens, and in this way you will fulfill the law of Christ. If anyone thinks he is something when he is nothing, he deceives himself."

GALATIANS 6:1-3

57

Jesus,

With this world full of temptations and the fact that ____ is bombarded on a daily basis with opportunity to turn his back on you and just live like the world says to live—please be strong in him. Help _____ to encourage others who have messed up that they can find forgiveness and be restored. Then please also protect _____ from giving in to the ways of the world so that he can fulfill your law and be a good witness for you in what he says and what he does...

"'These people honor me with their lips, but their hearts are far from me. They worship me in vain; their teachings are but rules taught by men.'" Jesus called the crowd to him and said, "Listen and understand. What goes into a man's mouth does not make him 'unclean,' but what comes out of his mouth, that is what makes him 'unclean.'"

MATTHEW 15:8-11

58

Lord Jesus,

In a world that has lost its sense of honor—let _____ be a man of honor. Not just to the authority over him on earth but to you Lord. May he never be like those who honored you with their lips but who's hearts were far from you. Keep _____'s heart close to you and may his worship of you never be in vain. As the things that come out of the mouth make a person unclean—keep _____ clean before you as you put a guard over his tongue...

* **H O N O R** *

"And over all these virtues put on love, which binds them all together in perfect unity. Let the peace of Christ rule in your hearts, since as members of one body you were called to peace. And be thankful."

COLOSSIANS 3:14-15

59

Father,

Sometimes there are challenges to being part of a team. There are so many different personalities and so much time spent together. be with ____ as he manages all that it means to be part of a larger group of athletes. Help him to choose love for his teammates and coaches so that they can be bound together in unity as they work together this season. Let the peace of Christ rule in _____'s heart since you have called him to peace so that they can work together and accomplish big goals...

* U N I T Y *

"But when he, the Spirit of truth, comes, he will guide you into all truth. He will not speak on his own; he will speak only what he hears, and he will tell you what is yet to come."

JOHN 16:13

60

Lord,

Thank you for the Spirit of Truth. Send him _____'s way and guide ____ in all that he faces today. Please continue to speak truth and wisdom that comes from you as you give _____ clarity to make the decisions he has to make. So many choices he deals with are huge and can have lasting consequences so please pour out your Spirit of truth and give _____ ears to hear and strength to obey...

"I keep asking that the God of our Lord Jesus Christ, the glorious Father, may give you the Spirit of wisdom and revelation, so that you may know him better. I pray also that the eyes of your heart may be enlightened in order that you may know the hope to which he has called you, the riches of his glorious inheritance in the saints, and his incomparably great power for us who believe. That power is like the working of his mighty strength, which he exerted in Christ when he raised him from the dead and seated him at his right hand in the heavenly realms, far above all rule and authority, power and dominion, and every title that can be given, not only in the present age but also in the one to come."

EPHESIANS 1:17-21

61

Lord God,

Would you give ____ the Spirit of wisdom and revelation so that he may know you better? Also please enlighten the eyes of his heart so that he can know the hope to which you have called him and the riches of his glorious inheritance in the saints and especially that he can know your incomparably great power that you exert for those who believe. Thank you that your power is like the working of your mighty strength that you exerted in Christ when you raised him from the dead and seated him at your right hand far above all rule and authority, power and dominion and any title that can be given---your power is so great Lord and I'm grateful that you show it in behalf of ____. Let him see you and experience you today in the face of all the challenges he has ahead. Be strong in him...

* CHALLENGES *

"For all have sinned and fall short of the glory of God, and are justified by his grace as a gift, through the redemption that is in Christ Jesus."

ROMANS 3:23-24 (ESV)

62

Father God,

When _____ feels like a failure for whatever reason. Don't let him listen to the voices that tell him the negative things but let him look to you and your truth and focus on what you say when you tell him that ALL have sinned and fall short of your glory. Thank you for promising that you will justify _____ by faith as a gift when he trusts in you because he has been redeemed by the blood of Jesus. Instead of hanging his head and living in defeat, Lord, let him stand tall knowing that as your child he is redeemed and forgiven...

* **S I N** *

"May the God who gives endurance and encouragement give you a spirit of unity among yourselves as you follow Christ Jesus, so that with one heart and mouth you may glorify the God and Father of our Lord Jesus Christ. Accept one another, then, just as Christ accepted you, in order to bring praise to God."

ROMANS 15:5-7

63

God,

You know how intense things can get on a team fighting to be successful during the season especially. I know it can be tough on ___ sometimes so please continue to give him endurance and encouragement so that he can be in a spirit of unity with his fellow players and coaches. Let _____ follow Jesus so that he can be one who brings you glory and use ____ to help other players feel accepted and part of the team no matter their position or ability level all in order that he would bring praise to your name and make you famous to those around him...

* T E A M M A T E S *

"For this reason, since the day we heard about you, we have not stopped praying for you and asking God to fill you with the knowledge of his will through all spiritual wisdom and understanding. And we pray this in order that you may live a life worthy of the Lord and may please him in every way: bearing fruit in every good work, growing in the knowledge of God, being strengthened with all power according to his glorious might so that you may have great endurance and patience, and joyfully giving thanks to the Father, who has qualified you to share in the inheritance of the saints in the kingdom of light."

COLOSSIANS 1:9-12

64

Father god,

Would you please fill _____ with the knowledge of your will through all spiritual wisdom and understanding? I ask this so that he may live a life worthy of you and may please you in every good way as he bears fruit through good work, as he plays the game you've gifted him to do. let him grow in his knowledge of you. Strengthen _____ with all power according to your glorious might so that he may have great endurance and patience and joyfully give you thanks because you have qualified him to share in the inheritance of the saints in the kingdom of light...

* **STRENGTH** *

"For our light and momentary troubles are achieving for us an eternal glory that far outweighs them all. So we fix our eyes not on what is seen, but on what is unseen. For what is seen is temporary, but what is unseen is eternal."

2 CORINTHIANS 4:17-18

65

Lord Jesus,

Life can get tough in the world of athletics with the pressure to perform and succeed. Help _____ recognize that these troubles are not eternal and that they can produce an eternal glory which far outweighs the here and now. Let _____ fix his eyes not on what is seen but on what is unseen because those are the things that are eternal and the things that truly last. Use these temporary challenges to shape _____'s character into what you want it to be so that you can use him for your glory and purposes...

"Be very careful, then, how you live--not as unwise but as wise, making the most of every opportunity, because the days are evil. Therefore do not be foolish, but understand what the Lord's will is. Do not get drunk on wine, which leads to debauchery. Instead, be filled with the Spirit."

EPHESIANS 5:15-18

66

Lord Jesus,

No matter what choices he is surrounded by let _____ be very careful how he lives not as unwise but as wise so that he makes the most of every opportunity you give him because these days are evil. Lord do not let him be foolish but understand what your will is. Keep _____ from getting drunk on wine or alcohol which leads to debauchery but Father instead fill him with your Holy Spirit so that he makes the best choices possible in every situation...

"And my God will meet all your needs according to his glorious riches in Christ Jesus. To our God and Father be glory for ever and ever. Amen."

Philippians 4:19-20

67

Father,

Although there is a strong temptation to trust in self and look to the things of the world for what he needs, open _____'s eyes to the truth that you are what he needs most. Thank you for promising to supply all of _____'s needs according to your glorious riches in Christ Jesus. Always let him look to you first and to trust that you have his best plans in your mind. I praise you for loving ____ and providing for his every need...

"Not that I have already obtained all this, or have already been made perfect, but I press on to take hold of that for which Christ Jesus took hold of me. Brothers, I do not consider myself yet to have taken hold of it. But one thing I do: Forgetting what is behind and straining toward what is ahead, I press on toward the goal to win the prize for which God has called me heavenward in Christ Jesus. "

PHILIPPIANS 3:12-14

68

O Lord,

I know that _____ has not achieved perfection at all but inspire him to press on to make it his own because Christ Jesus has made him his own. When things don't go perfect for ____ let him forget what lies behind and strain forward to what lies ahead as he presses on toward the goal for the prize of the upward call of you in Christ Jesus. Make your calling known in _____'s life and keep his eyes focused on the prize of being obedient to you. Don't let him get caught up in the wrong kinds of goals but stay the course that you have set before him...

* **G O A L** *

"Though I walk in the midst of trouble, you preserve my life; you stretch out your hand against the anger of my foes, with your right hand you save me. The LORD will fulfill [his purpose] for me; your love, O LORD, endures forever-- do not abandon the works of your hands."

PSALM 138:7-8

69

Father God,

Thank you that though _____ often walks in the midst of trouble, stress, persecution and attack that you preserve his life. Thank you for stretching out your hand against the anger of his foes and save him. Lord would you continue to fulfill your purpose for _____. I praise you O Lord that your love endures forever and you do not abandon the work of your hands. Hold _____ close in your hands today...

"You were taught, with regard to your former way of life, to put off your old self, which is being corrupted by its deceitful desires; to be made new in the attitude of your minds; and to put on the new self, created to be like God in true righteousness and holiness."

EPHESIANS 4:22-24

70

Jesus,

It is through your death on the cross that new life was made available to us-thank you. Would you help _____ to keep on putting off his old self that is continually being corrupted by its deceitful desires and make him new in the attitude of his mind. Let _____ put on the new self that was created to be like God in true righteousness and holiness as he lives for you in this world that offers him every other option. Give him wisdom to lay aside the old self and choose the new self today...

"O God, you are my God, earnestly I seek you; my soul thirsts for you, my body longs for you, in a dry and weary land where there is no water."

PSALM 63:1

71

Lord,

Thank you for being god and not leaving _____ on his own in the challenges he faces regularly. Give _____ a desire to seek after you earnestly to the point that he thirsts for you like a man in a dry and desperate desert because you promise that when we seek after you that we will find you-- so be found by _____ let him never settle for less than a full relationship with you...

"But seek first his kingdom and his righteousness, and all these things will be given to you as well. "

MATTHEW 6:33

72

O Lord,

You know how this world is and how athletes like _____ are told such different messages about what to focus on and where to spend his time and energy. Keep _____ motivated to seek after you first. To seek your kingdom first and then to recognize and trust that you will take care of all the other things. Give him freedom in his mind to let you handle all the details of his life and to be okay with not necessarily knowing every next step but to trust that you do know and that you have great plans for him if he will seek you and trust you...

* B A L A N C E *

"This is love for God: to obey his commands. And his commands are not burdensome, for everyone born of God overcomes the world. This is the victory that has overcome the world, even our faith."

1 JOHN 5:3-4

73

Lord God,

As a competitor, you know that _____ always plays to win and wants to overcome whatever opponent he faces. You Lord are the ultimate victor and your victories have such eternal results. Help _____ see the reality of the victory that comes when he chooses to obey your commands. Thank you that your commands are not burdensome because those who are born of God overcome the world. Thank you for that faith and the victory to overcome the world. Let _____ be an overcomer today...

* **O V E R C O M E** *

"Reckless words pierce like a sword, but the tongue of the wise brings healing. Truthful lips endure forever, but a lying tongue lasts only a moment. There is deceit in the hearts of those who plot evil, but joy for those who promote peace."

PROVERBS 12:18-20

74

Father,

Teammates spend so much time together in all kinds of situations and it's easy to let their tongues get away from them. Let _____ remember that reckless words pierce like a sword but the tongue of the wise brings healing while truthful lips endure forever but a lying tongue lasts only a moment. Encourage _____ to choose a wise tongue as he interacts with others and to avoid the deceit in the hearts of those who plot evil. Thank you that there is joy for those who promote peace. Let _____ experience that joy...

* T R U T H *

"But you, man of God, flee from all this, and pursue righteousness, godliness, faith, love, endurance and gentleness. Fight the good fight of the faith. Take hold of the eternal life to which you were called when you made your good confession in the presence of many witnesses."

TIMOTHY 6:11-12

75

Lord God,

With options all around him to give in to the opportunities of the moment, call _____ as a man of God to flee from the ways of this world and to pursue righteousness, godliness, faith, love, endurance and gentleness. Strengthen him to fight the good fight of faith and to take hold of the eternal life to which you have called him when he made his confession of faith...

"We put no stumbling block in anyone's path, so that our ministry will not be discredited. Rather, as servants of God we commend ourselves in every way: in great endurance; in troubles, hardships and distresses; in beatings, imprisonments and riots; in hard work, sleepless nights and hunger; in purity, understanding, patience and kindness; in the Holy Spirit and in sincere love."

2 CORINTHIANS 6:3-6

76

Father God,

Please let _____ avoid being any type of stumbling block to
others so that his ministry will not be discredited.
As a servant of God give him great endurance in
troubles, hardships, distresses, beatings, hard work,
sleepless nights, hunger, purity, understanding, patience
and kindness through the Holy Spirit and in sincere love.
Don't let the troubles that come all around get him down
but keep ____ focused on the call you have on his life and
let others see that he is different because he
loves you and lives for you...

* H A R D S H I P S *

"I pray that out of his glorious riches he may strengthen you with power through his Spirit in your inner being, so that Christ may dwell in your hearts through faith. And I pray that you, being rooted and established in love, may have power, together with all the saints, to grasp how wide and long and high and deep is the love of Christ, and to know this love that surpasses knowledge--that you may be filled to the measure of all the fullness of God."

EPHESIANS 3:14-19

77

Father,

I pray that out of your glorious riches you will strengthen _____ with power through your Spirit in his inner being so that Christ may dwell in his heart through faith. Also Lord let ____ be rooted and established in love so that he has power together with the saints to grasp how wide and long and high and deep is the love of Christ. Then let him know the love that surpasses knowledge and be filled to the measure of all fullness of God...

"I have fought the good fight, I have finished the race, I have kept the faith. Now there is in store for me the crown of righteousness, which the Lord, the righteous Judge, will award to me on that day--and not only to me, but also to all who have longed for his appearing."

2 TIMOTHY 4:7-8

78

Lord God,

There are so many battles that _____ has to face. Would you fill him so that after the battles he can say that he has fought the good fight, finished the race and kept the faith? Thank you that you can strengthen him for the fight and that you have the crown of righteousness that you as the righteous judge will award on that day. Let ____ stay focused on relying on you as his power and strength for every battle...

* **B A T T L E** *

"For by the grace given me I say to every one of you: Do not think of yourself more highly than you ought, but rather think of yourself with sober judgment, in accordance with the measure of faith God has given you."

ROMANS 12:3

"Toward the scorners he is scornful, but to the humble he gives favor."

PROVERBS 3:34 (ESV)

79

Lord Jesus,

Although people tend to look differently at athletes and put them on pedestals, help _____ to never think of himself more highly than he ought but rather to think of himself with sober judgment in accordance with the measure of faith you have given him. Remind ____ that you scorn the scornful but give favor to the humble. Let him be worthy of your favor...

"For I know the plans I have for you,"
declares the LORD, "plans to prosper
you and not to harm you, plans to give
you hope and a future. Then you will call
upon me and come and pray to me, and
I will listen to you. You will seek me and
find me when you seek me with all your
heart."

JEREMIAH 29:11-13

80

O Lord,

Thank you that you know the plans you have for _____.
Thank you that those plans are to prosper him not to
harm him and you want to give him a hope and a future.
Let _____ rest in that knowledge and learn to call on you
and come and pray to you. I praise you that you listen to
his prayers. Give ____ a desire to seek you and realize the
promise that when he does seek you that he will find you...

"Likewise, you who are younger, be subject to the elders. Clothe yourselves, all of you, with humility toward one another, for "God opposes the proud but gives grace to the humble."

1 Peter 5:5 (ESV)

81

Lord Jesus,

Be with _____ as he deals with coaches, teaches, trainers and others who lead him. Give him the respect that those who are younger should have for those who are older. Let _____ clothe himself with humility towards others since you oppose the proud but give grace to the humble. Don't let _____ set himself up to be opposed by you but rather let him set himself up to receive your grace by the way he conducts himself with humility and grace...

AUTHORITY

"But the eyes of the LORD are on those who fear him, on those whose hope is in his unfailing love, to deliver them from death and keep them alive in famine. We wait in hope for the LORD; he is our help and our shield. In him our hearts rejoice, for we trust in his holy name. May your unfailing love rest upon us, O LORD, even as we put our hope in you. "

PSALM 33:18-22

82

O Lord,

Thank you that your eyes are on _____ today. Let him continue to fear and respect you as you deserve and to set his hope on your unfailing love knowing that you will deliver him from circumstances that are designed to destroy him and that you will provide for his needs. Let _____ wait in hope for you as his help and shield. Let his heart rejoice in you as he trusts in your holy name. Let your unfailing love rest on _____ Lord as he puts his hope in you...

"Be imitators of God, therefore, as dearly loved children and live a life of love, just as Christ loved us and gave himself up for us as a fragrant offering and sacrifice to God."

EPHESIANS 5:1-2

83

Heavenly Father,

When _____ begins to feel down on himself or focused on his failings and weaknesses, remind him that he is your child. Thank you that you love _____ dearly to the point that Jesus died for him. Let _____ always remember his relationship with you and his value in your sight. May his life be like that of Jesus- a fragrant offering and sacrifice to you god...

"Keep me safe, O God, for in you I take refuge. I said to the LORD, "You are my Lord; apart from you I have no good thing."

PSALM 16:1-2

84

O god,

There are so many things and people that we are tempted to place our trust in and so many people and things that are coming against _____. Father keep him safe. Be his refuge in all things. Help _____ to recognize that you are his protector and his refuge and that apart from you there is no good thing. Watch over _____ as he goes through the physically demanding and emotionally draining life of athletics. Be there for him and let him see you...

"Love must be sincere. Hate what is evil; cling to what is good. Be devoted to one another in brotherly love. Honor one another above yourselves. Never be lacking in zeal, but keep your spiritual fervor, serving the Lord. Be joyful in hope, patient in affliction, faithful in prayer. Share with God's people who are in need."

ROMANS 12:9-13

85

Dear God,

Let _____ be one who has a sincere love, who hates what is evil and clings to what is good. Be with his team and let them be devoted to each other in brotherly love. Lead _____ to set an example of honoring each other above self. Never let ___ be lacking in zeal but keep his spiritual fervor strong as he serves you. Let him be joyful in hope, patient in affliction and faithful in prayer. Use ____ to share with your people who are in need...

"Flee from sexual immorality. All other sins a man commits are outside his body, but he who sins sexually sins against his own body. Do you not know that your body is a temple of the Holy Spirit, who is in you, whom you have received from God? You are not your own; you were bought at a price. Therefore honor God with your body."

1 Corinthians 6:18-2

86

Lord Jesus,

With temptation all around him let _____ learn to flee from sexual immorality that is sin against his own body. Let _____ remember that his body is the temple of your Holy Spirit that he received from you. As athletes take care of their bodies physically in order to compete, don't let _____ ever overlook the fact that his body is not his but that he was bought with a price and therefore let him honor you with his body in all things by exerting self control and making wise choices...

"Be strong and courageous. Do not be afraid or terrified because of them, for the LORD your God goes with you; he will never leave you nor forsake you."

Deuteronomy 31:6

87

God,

You know how many opportunities _____ has to face very difficult circumstances and opponents who are out to destroy him, please let _____ be strong and courageous no matter what. Don't let fear or terror overwhelm _____ but keep him calm and trusting in you because he knows that you are with him wherever he goes. Thank you that you will never leave ____ or forsake him and let that Truth strengthen him to stand firm and do what you've called him to do regardless of the situation...

"Dear friends, do not be surprised at the painful trial you are suffering, as though something strange were happening to you. But rejoice that you participate in the sufferings of Christ, so that you may be overjoyed when his glory is revealed. If you are insulted because of the name of Christ, you are blessed, for the Spirit of glory and of God rests on you."

1 Peter 4:12-14

88

Father,

I know that sometimes as a believer following after you _____ will be persecuted for his faith. Let him not be surprised at the painful trials he faces but let ____ rejoice in the sufferings of Christ so that he may be overjoyed when your glory is revealed. Thank you that whenever _____ faces insults or ridicule because of the name of Christ that he is blessed because the Spirit of glory and God rests on him...

"For it is commendable if a man bears up under the pain of unjust suffering because he is conscious of God."

1 PETER 2:19

89

Lord God,

It hurts when life isn't fair and things are not going well. When _____ faces situations that cause him to suffer unjustly whether he is blamed for something not his fault or accused of something someone else did or anything else— God let him bear up under it because he knows he is yours. Guard his tongue in those times and let him be comforted by knowing the truth and being man of integrity...

"In fact, everyone who wants to live a godly life in Christ Jesus will be persecuted, while evil men and impostors will go from bad to worse, deceiving and being deceived. But as for you, continue in what you have learned and have become convinced of, because you know those from whom you learned it, and how from infancy you have known the holy Scriptures, which are able to make you wise for salvation through faith in Christ Jesus. All Scripture is God-breathed and is useful for teaching, rebuking, correcting and training in righteousness, so that the man of God may be thoroughly equipped for every good work."

2 TIMOTHY 3:12-17

90

Lord,

Increase _____'s desire to live a godly life in Christ Jesus even though it will mean persecution as evil people and impostors go from bad to worse deceiving and being deceived. God you are more powerful than these evil people and you can encourage _____ to continue in what he has firmly believed as he continues knowing you and your Word. Thank you that your Word is able to make _____ wise for salvation through faith in Jesus Christ. Use your Word in ____'s life to teach, discipline, correct and train him in righteousness that he may be a man of God, complete and equipped for every good work...

"The LORD bless you and keep you; the LORD make his face shine upon you and be gracious to you; the LORD turn his face toward you and give you peace."

Numbers 6:24-26

91

Father,

Thank you that you care about every aspect of ____'s life and that you know the things that come at him that are designed to steal his peace and create turmoil in his life. Please bless _____ and keep him. Let your face shone on him and be gracious to him. Lord turn your face toward _____ and give him peace as he puts his faith in you and refuses to give in to the pressure the world throws at him...

PROTECTION

"So do not be ashamed to testify about our Lord, or ashamed of me his prisoner. But join with me in suffering for the gospel, by the power of God, who has saved us and called us to a holy life--not because of anything we have done but because of his own purpose and grace. This grace was given us in Christ Jesus before the beginning of time, but it has now been revealed through the appearing of our Savior, Christ Jesus, who has destroyed death and has brought life and immortality to light through the gospel."

2 Timothy 1:8-10

92

Lord Jesus,

You stood strong in the face of opposition and challenge, help _____ to never be ashamed of your Gospel even if it means that he shares in your suffering. Give him your power not because of his works but because you have called him and you have a purpose for him through Jesus before the ages began. Thank you that your purpose has been manifested through Jesus' life and death as he brought immortality to light through the Gospel. Let _____ be motivated by his faith to stand firm in whatever he faces today...

"Let the peace of Christ rule in your hearts, since as members of one body you were called to peace. And be thankful. Let the word of Christ dwell in you richly as you teach and admonish one another with all wisdom, and as you sing psalms, hymns and spiritual songs with gratitude in your hearts to God. And whatever you do, whether in word or deed, do it all in the name of the Lord Jesus, giving thanks to God the Father through him. "

COLOSSIANS 3:15-17

93

Lord Jesus,

Peace is not something that is abounding in _____'s life as
an athlete. Instead of focusing on negatives or on
stressful thoughts, let the peace of Christ rule in his
heart as he was called to. Let _____ be thankful and let
your Word dwell in him richly, teaching and admonishing
him in all wisdom with thankfulness to god. Lord
whatever _____ does whether in word or deed let him do
everything in the name of the Lord Jesus Christ giving
thanks to god the Father through Jesus...

"I thank my God every time I remember you. In all my prayers for all of you, I always pray with joy because of your partnership in the gospel from the first day until now, being confident of this, that he who began a good work in you will carry it on to completion until the day of Christ Jesus."

PHILIPPIANS 1:3-6

94

Father,

I am so grateful for the gift of _____. Thank you for blessing me with him in my life and for the joy that brings to me. Today would you continue your work in _____? Thank you that I can be confident that you will never leave him or desert him but that you who began a good work in him will certainly carry it on to completion. Let _____ realize that you are doing a great work in his life and that you will complete what you have started in your time according to your plan. I praise you that ____'s future is secure in you...

* F U T U R E *

"Therefore, there is now no condemnation for those who are in Christ Jesus, because through Christ Jesus the law of the Spirit of life set me free from the law of sin and death."

ROMANS 8:1-2

95

Lord,

Thank you that there is no condemnation for those who are in Christ Jesus. Thank you that the law of the Spirit has set _____ free from the law of sin and death. Let _____ understand this freedom and live in it instead of under the condemnation that he might be burdened with from others when things don't go perfectly. Father when he messes up help _____ realize that he can confess and repent and be restored to relationship with you. Thank you that you do not expect perfection from _____ but you offer grace and mercy...

"The LORD is a refuge for the oppressed, a stronghold in times of trouble."

PSALM 9:9

"Cast your cares on the LORD and he will sustain you; he will never let the righteous fall."

PSALM 55:22

96

O Lord,

In challenging times when _____feels like he is all alone and no one else is on his side let him be reminded that you are there for him. Thank you for being a refuge for the oppressed and a stronghold in times of trouble. Please continue to show this truth to ____ so that he will become quick to cast all his cares on you so that you can sustain him. I praise you that you will never let the righteous fall. Count _____ as one of your righteous and uphold him with your mighty hand...

"Listen to my prayer, O God, do not ignore my plea; hear me and answer me. My thoughts trouble me and I am distraught at the voice of the enemy, at the stares of the wicked; for they bring down suffering upon me and revile me in their anger."

PSALM 55:1-3

97

O god,

I know sometimes _____ has troubling thoughts and that
he can get distraught at the voice of the enemy and the
stares of the wicked that he has to deal with on an
ongoing basis. Those enemies want to bring down suffering
on him and revile him in their anger. When he feels the
heat from his many enemies let him call out to you and
know that you will hear his prayer. Thank you Lord for
listening and not ignoring _____'s pleas. I praise you that
you want _____ to bring his prayers to you and that you will
answer...

"This calls for patient endurance on the part of the saints who obey God's commandments and remain faithful to Jesus."

REVELATION 14:12

98

God,

In this day of instant everything, give _____ the patient endurance he needs to obey your commandments even if there is not a visible, immediate reaction. Keep _____ close to you and inspire him to remain faithful to Jesus in everything he does. Give him wisdom to see that obeying your commandments has far lasting positive consequences that are worth the endurance it takes to realize them. Don't let _____ give in to the mentality that says to grab what you want and not worry about anything beyond the pleasure of the moment...

* P A T I E N C E *

"But a time is coming, and has come, when you will be scattered, each to his own home. You will leave me all alone. Yet I am not alone, for my Father is with me. I have told you these things, so that in me you may have peace. In this world you will have trouble. But take heart! I have overcome the world."

JOHN 16:32-33

99

Father,

Thank you for being with _____. On days when he feels alone for whatever reason, remind him that you are there and you are with him. Thank you that peace comes with knowing you are present-bring peace into _____'s life today. Although he faces tribulation and tough things, still you are with him. Let him feel your presence in the face of what he is facing and let that cause him to take heart because you-O mighty God, have overcome the world. Don't let _____ get down when circumstances don't go his way with practice or games or life. Thank you that you are on _____'s side and you will overcome what he is dealing with when he finds his strength in you...

* **OVERCOME** *

"It is for freedom that Christ has set us free. Stand firm, then, and do not let yourselves be burdened again by a yoke of slavery."

GALATIANS 5:1

100

Father,

It is easy to get caught up in bondage to sin and self through wrong thinking, guilt and shame. Please don't ever let ____ think that he has to continue in sin because he has already been involved in it. Thank you that it was for freedom that you set _____ free in Christ Jesus. Let that be a continual encouragement to _____ to stand firm and not let himself be burdened again by a yoke of slavery. Give _____ a passion to live in your freedom and help others to know that same freedom.

* F R E E D O M *

"Therefore do not worry about tomorrow, for tomorrow will worry about itself. Each day has enough trouble of its own."

MATTHEW 6:34

101

Lord Jesus,

   With so many pressures and people coming at _____ consistently, keep him from being anxious about tomorrow. Thank you that you have given him everything he needs to live this life and don't let him borrow trouble from one day to the next but deal with each day as it comes as he

   trusts in you. Help _____ trust and rest in you today...

* **W O R R Y** *

"But make up your mind not to worry beforehand how you will defend your-selves. For I will give you words and wis-dom that none of your adversaries will be able to resist or contradict. You will be betrayed even by parents, brothers, relatives and friends, and they will put some of you to death. All men will hate you because of me. But not a hair of your head will perish. By standing firm you will gain life."

LUKE 21:14-19

102

O god,

You know how hard it can be to listen to people attack or criticize and _____ has to face that regularly. Father help him not to focus on defending himself but to trust in you. Please give him the right words to say at the right times even when facing the pain of betrayal. As athletes enjoy success they also have opportunity to deal with lots of criticism. Give him grace and wisdom to know who to listen to and when to ignore. Remind ____ of who he is in you and encourage him daily. Let him stand firm in the face of whatever comes against him according to your power at work...

* E N D U R A N C E *

"So, if you think you are standing firm, be careful that you don't fall! No temptation has seized you except what is common to man. And God is faithful; he will not let you be tempted beyond what you can bear. But when you are tempted, he will also provide a way out so that you can stand up under it."

1 CORINTHIANS 10:12-13

103

Jesus,

There is no end to the opportunities _____ faces to give in to sin. Even when he makes the right choices and thinks he can stand, remind _____ to always take heed lest he fall. Thank you that there is no temptation ____ will ever face that is not common to man. I praise you for being faithful in _____'s life and please do not let him be tempted beyond his ability. Let _____ find the way of escape that you provide so that he can endure the temptations that come his way...

TEMPTATION

"Let us not become weary in doing good, for at the proper time we will reap a harvest if we do not give up. Therefore, as we have opportunity, let us do good to all people, especially to those who belong to the family of believers."

GALATIANS 6:9-10

104

Lord Jesus,

It can be so tough and exhausting even keeping up with _____'s schedule. When he gets worn out physically and mentally he may wonder why it matters. Do not let _____ grow weary of doing good even if he is the only one doing good and even if he is not seeing any positive results from obeying you in the moment. Thank you that in due season you will allow him to reap the rewards of following you if he doesn't give up. As he has opportunity, let him do good to everyone and especially to those in the household of faith. Strengthen the team as they each learn to build each other up and work together to be all they can be...

"Come to me, all you who are weary and burdened, and I will give you rest. Take my yoke upon you and learn from me, for I am gentle and humble in heart, and you will find rest for your souls. For my yoke is easy and my burden is light."

MATTHEW 11:28-30

105

O Lord,

You know how much pressure _____ is under as an athlete trying to manage school, practice, training and life in general. I know he gets weary and tired as he labors to be the best he can be. Thank you for calling _____ to come

to you. I pray that he will turn to you first when he is exhausted and feeling burdened so that you can give him the rest he needs. Let _____ take your yoke upon himself and learn from you for you are gentle and lowly in heart and he can find rest for his soul. Thank you that your yoke is easy and your burden is light. That is so vastly different from the world he lives in. Let him find peace in you today...

* **T I R E D** *

"No weapon forged against you will prevail, and you will refute every tongue that accuses you. This is the heritage of the servants of the LORD, and this is their vindication from me," declares the LORD."

Isaiah 54:17

106

Almighty god,

Thank you that no weapon formed against _____ will prevail and that you will refute every tongue that accuses him. There is no shortage of people who are waiting to share their opinion about ____ and his performance at any given time. Let him trust you and not listen to the things they say against him because this is the heritage that he has as a servant of your Lord and you alone can vindicate him. Bless ____ today as only you can...

* B L E S S I N G *

"Do you not know that in a race all the runners run, but only one receives the prize? So run that you may obtain it. Every athlete exercises self-control in all things. They do it to receive a perishable wreath, but we an imperishable. So I do not run aimlessly; I do not box as one beating the air. But I discipline my body and keep it under control, lest after preaching to others I myself should be disqualified."

1 Corinthians 9:24-27 (ESV)

107

Lord,

Your word says that in a race all runner run but only one receives the prize. I know _____ has learned so much about competing and working hard and doing his best. Please continue to inspire him to run so that he may obtain the prize. As an athlete, help _____ exercise self control in all things because it is worth it to focus on the imperishable prize as opposed to the ones who perish. Remind _____that he does not run as one who is aimless or as one who boxes the air but he disciplines his body and keeps it under control so that after preaching to others and being a witness for the gospel that he would not be disqualified even when it seems like he might be the only one making wise choices, remind him of the value of obeying your Word...

* D I S C I P L I N E *

" I know what it is to be in need, and I know what it is to have plenty. I have learned the secret of being content in any and every situation, whether well fed or hungry, whether living in plenty or in want. I can do everything through him who gives me strength."

PHILIPPIANS 4:12-13

108

Lord,

You know that _____ has experienced ups and downs in his athletic career. Would you help him to say like Paul that he knows what it is to be in need and to have plenty? Teach him the secret of being content in any and every situation whether good or bad, whether well fed or hungry, whether living in plenty or want. Reinforce to _____ the truth behind how he can handle his every different type of circumstance with grace and that is recognizing that he can do all things through you who gives him strength. Thank you that you are the strength he needs...

"That is why I am suffering as I am. Yet I am not ashamed, because I know whom I have believed, and am convinced that he is able to guard what I have entrusted to him for that day. What you heard from me, keep as the pattern of sound teaching, with faith and love in Christ Jesus. Guard the good deposit that was entrusted to you--guard it with the help of the Holy Spirit who lives in us. "

2 Timothy 1:12-14

109

Lord,

Thank you that you uphold those who are unashamed of you. Would you give _____ that kind of faith? The kind of faith that says "I am not ashamed" because he knows whom he has believed in. God let ____ continue be convinced that you will guard what you've entrusted to him in the place you have him right now and help him to follow the pattern of sound words that he has learned from Scripture as he goes about his daily life. Grow ___'s faith and love thru the Holy Spirit and please continue to guard his very life so that you can use him...

"But among you there must not be even a hint of sexual immorality, or of any kind of impurity, or of greed, because these are improper for God's holy people. Nor should there be obscenity, foolish talk or coarse joking, which are out of place, but rather thanksgiving. For of this you can be sure: No immoral, impure or greedy person--such a man is an idolater--has any inheritance in the kingdom of Christ and of God."

EPHESIANS 5:3-5

110

Lord God,

All kinds of opportunities come ____'s way. Please keep him from even a hint of sexual immorality or any type of impurity or of greed because these are improper for your holy people. Also keep ____ from obscenity, foolish talk and coarse joking-- which are out of place but help him be thankful in what he says and does. Let ____ see that immorality, impurity and greed cause one to become an idolater and keep people from their inheritance in your kingdom. Rather let ____ make wise choices that keep him on the path to receiving the inheritance you have for him...

"Be still, and know that I am God; I will be exalted among the nations, I will be exalted in the earth." The LORD Almighty is with us; the God of Jacob is our fortress."

Psalm 46:10-11

111

Lord Jesus,

With so little time to stop and rest or even think, let _____ find time to be still and know that you are God. Let him exalt you among the nations and on the earth. I praise you that you are that God—the One who will be exalted! Thank you that you are with _____ and that you —the God of Jacob are his fortress and a place of peace for him in the chaos of life. Speak peace into his heart today no matter what is happening around him...

"In the beginning was the Word, and the Word was with God, and the Word was God. He was with God in the beginning. Through him all things were made; without him nothing was made that has been made. In him was life, and that life was the light of men. The light shines in the darkness, but the darkness has not understood it."

JOHN 1:1-5

112

Lord Jesus,

You were there in the beginning. You are the Word itself and you were with God at the start. Thank you that all things were made through you and in you is life. Thank you that that life is the light of men and that it shines in the darkness. So often it can feel dark around _____. Thank you for being the light in his world and I praise you that your light overcomes the darkness. Never let _____ get to the place where he feels the darkness is winning but let him cling to this truth that you are the light and you overcome...

"Blessed is the man who remains steadfast under trial, for when he has stood the test he will receive the crown of life, which God has promised to those who love him. Let no one say when he is tempted, "I am being tempted by God," for God cannot be tempted with evil, and he himself tempts no one. But each person is tempted when he is lured and enticed by his own desire. Then desire when it has conceived gives birth to sin, and sin when it is fully grown brings forth death."

JAMES 1:12-15 (ESV)

113

Lord Jesus,

Please help _____ to remain steadfast under trials that will come his way. Bless him for standing firm and let him receive the crown of life you have promised to those who love you. Don't let _____ ever say or believe that he is being tempted by you because you cannot be tempted with evil nor do you tempt anyone, but let _____ recognize that when he is tempted that he is being lured and enticed by his own desire and let him see how dangerous that desire can be as it leads from desire to sin that leads to broken fellowship with you. Keep _____ close to you and help him to see sin and temptation for what they really are and to resist the temptations by your power at work in him.

TEMPTATIONS

"Be on your guard; stand firm in the faith; be men of courage; be strong."

1 CORINTHIANS 16:13

114

Lord,

With so many people speaking into _____'s life and so many opportunities to give in to the desires of the world—its more necessary than ever that you keep _____ on his guard. Let him be super aware of where the dangers are for him. Strengthen _____ to stand firm in his faith. Fill him with courage because he trusts in you. Let _____ do what others might not be willing to do as a man of courage. Finally help _____ to be strong, whether it is to do the right things or not do the wrong things, give him the strength to make wise, courageous decisions...

"It does not, therefore, depend on man's desire or effort, but on God's mercy. For the Scripture says to Pharaoh: "I raised you up for this very purpose, that I might display my power in you and that my name might be proclaimed in all the earth."

ROMANS 9:16-17

115

Father God,

Thank you that nothing depends on man's effort but on your mercy. Thank you that you raised _____ up for your purpose so that you might display your power through him and that your name might be proclaimed in all the earth. Do something in and through _____ that only you can do and remind him to rely on your strength not his own as he faces the challenges of this day...

"I am not ashamed of the gospel, because it is the power of God for the salvation of everyone who believes: first for the Jew, then for the Gentile. For in the gospel a righteousness from God is revealed, a righteousness that is by faith from first to last, just as it is written: "The righteous will live by faith."

ROMANS 1:16-17

116

Lord Jesus,

Never let _____ be ashamed of the Gospel because it is your power for the salvation of everyone who believes. Thank you that you reveal your righteousness through the Gospel as your people live by faith. Help _____ to live by faith even when he is competing and fighting to win the battles he faces. Let your power be his driving force and the only thing he trusts in. Let _____ choose to live his life in a way that is righteous and that reveals the Gospel to those around him in whatever ways you choose...

* **P O W E R** *

"Consider it pure joy, my brothers, whenever you face trials of many kinds, because you know that the testing of your faith develops perseverance. Perseverance must finish its work so that you may be mature and complete, not lacking anything."

James 1:2-4

117

Lord,

You know how things don't always go the way _____ wants them to on all kinds of levels. Help him to count it all joy when he faces trials of various kinds because he knows that the testing of his faith produces steadfastness. Let steadfastness have its full effect that _____ may be perfect and complete lacking in nothing. Continue to grow _____ into a man of God that stands for you in the face of anything...

* S T E A D Y *

"With this in mind, we constantly pray for you, that our God may count you worthy of his calling, and that by his power he may fulfill every good purpose of yours and every act prompted by your faith. We pray this so that the name of our Lord Jesus may be glorified in you, and you in him, according to the grace of our God and the Lord Jesus Christ."

2 THESSALONIANS 1:11-12

118

Almighty God,

Today I continue to pray that you will make _____ worthy
of his calling and I ask that he will fulfill every resolve
for good and every work of faith by your power. Let the
name of the Lord Jesus Christ be glorified in _____ and
you in him according to the grace of our God and the
Lord Jesus Christ. Thank you that you have the power to
make _____ worthy of your calling and I pray that he will
seek after you with all that he is...

"So do not throw away your confidence; it will be richly rewarded. You need to persevere so that when you have done the will of God, you will receive what he has promised."

HEBREWS 10:35-36

119

Father God,

Some circumstances try to rob _____ of his confidence. Let him never be shaken in his faith and belief that you are who you say you are. Empower _____ to persevere and to do your will so that he can receive what you've promised. Thank you that you promise to never leave ____ and to be with him no matter what. Let him rest in total assurance that you have good plans for him and that you will reward him for his perseverance. Thank you that your promises are always true and that no matter what happens in the day to day trials of athletics that _____ can be confident in you because he knows who He is in you...

"For even Christ did not please himself but, as it is written: "The insults of those who insult you have fallen on me." For everything that was written in the past was written to teach us, so that through endurance and the encouragement of the Scriptures we might have hope."

ROMANS 15:2-4

120

Lord,

Sometimes the pressure will get to _____ and he will feel like he isn't enough or he will begin to listen to the wrong voices that throw insults his way. In those moments let him look to Jesus-the One who was insulted falsely and yet did not sin or give up hope. Encourage _____ with the truth that through the endurance and strength he finds in your Word he can have hope to keep on living for you and doing the best he can for his team. Let him find his worth in who you say he is and not what anyone else says in the moments of pressure...

"For this reason I remind you to fan into flame the gift of God, which is in you through the laying on of my hands. For God did not give us a spirit of timidity, but a spirit of power, of love and of self-discipline."

2 TIMOTHY 1:6-7

121

O God,

You have uniquely gifted and equipped _____ for the life you have for him. Please fan into flame the gift of God that is in him through the presence of the Holy Spirit. Thank you that you did NOT give _____ a spirit of fear or timidity but a spirit of power and love and of self discipline. Let those characteristics grow in him and minister to others _____ comes in contact with. Don't let him listen to the voice of the enemy that tempts him to fear the unknown or the difficult but let your Spirit burn brightly in _____ so that fear has no place...

* **P A S S I O N** *

"But the fruit of the Spirit is love, joy, peace, patience, kindness, goodness, faithfulness, gentleness and self-control. Against such things there is no law. Those who belong to Christ Jesus have crucified the sinful nature with its passions and desires."

GALATIANS 5:22-24

122

Father God,

Thank you that you gave your Spirit to dwell in us. Would you fill _____ with your Holy Spirit today and let the fruit of your Spirit be evident in his life. Thank you that love, joy, peace, patience, kindness, goodness, faithfulness, gentleness and self control are possible even in the midst of crazy schedules, hard practices, demanding workouts and grueling games. Let ____ remember that he belongs to you and that you have crucified the flesh so that he can submit to your Spirit and not any fleshly desires. Use _____ to bring you glory and be a witness for you in everything he does...

* **P E A C E** *

"Do not let this Book of the Law depart from your mouth; meditate on it day and night, so that you may be careful to do everything written in it. Then you will be prosperous and successful. Have I not commanded you? Be strong and courageous. Do not be terrified; do not be discouraged, for the LORD your God will be with you wherever you go."

JOSHUA 1:8-9

123

Lord,

Thank you for your Word. Thank you for the Truth that is in it and please give ____ a passion for Scripture. Let him meditate on it and keep it in his mind so that he can be careful to do everything in it. Thank you that when _____ chooses to obey your Word that you will make him prosperous and successful. Also let ____ be strong and courageous because he is living in your power and might. Keep _____ from being terrified or intimidated by anything he faces and don't let him become discouraged because you are with him wherever he goes...

* C O U R A G E *

"But I will restore you to health and heal your wounds,' declares the LORD, 'because you are called an outcast, Zion for whom no one cares.'"

JEREMIAH 30:17

124

Jehovah Rapha,

You are the god who heals and I praise you for that. Thank you that you have the power to restore health and heal wounds. Would you demonstrate your healing power on _____'s life right now? Please restore his body to good health and bring healing to him. Let _____ look to you and trust that you have everything under your control...

"His divine power has given us everything we need for life and godliness through our knowledge of him who called us by his own glory and goodness. Through these he has given us his very great and precious promises, so that through them you may participate in the divine nature and escape the corruption in the world caused by evil desires. For this very reason, make every effort to add to your faith goodness; and to goodness, knowledge; and to knowledge, self-control; and to self-control, perseverance; and to perseverance, godliness; and to godliness, brotherly kindness; and to brotherly kindness, love. For if you possess these qualities in increasing measure, they will keep you from being ineffective and unproductive in your knowledge of our Lord Jesus Christ. "

2 PETER 1:3-8

125

Lord,

Thank you that your power has given _____ everything he needs for life and godliness through his knowledge of you who called him by your own glory and goodness. Through these let _____ realize your very great and precious promises so that through them _____ may participate in the divine nature and please let him escape the corruption of the world caused by evil desires. For this reason help _____ to add to his faith goodness and to goodness knowledge and to knowledge self control and to self control perseverance and to perseverance godliness and to godliness brotherly kindness and to brotherly kindness love. Thank you that when he possesses these qualities in increasing measure they will keep _____ from being ineffective and unproductive in his walk with you...

* **G O D L I N E S S** *

"This is the message we have heard from him and declare to you: God is light; in him there is no darkness at all. If we claim to have fellowship with him yet walk in the darkness, we lie and do not live by the truth. But if we walk in the light, as he is in the light, we have fellowship with one another, and the blood of Jesus, his Son, purifies us from all sin. If we claim to be without sin, we deceive ourselves and the truth is not in us. If we confess our sins, he is faithful and just and will forgive us our sins and purify us from all unrighteousness."

1 JOHN 1:5-9

126

Father God,

Thank you for the message you've given. Help _____ to always remember that you are light and in you is no darkness at all knowing that those who claim to be yours but who walk in the dark do not live by truth. Thank you that if _____ chooses to walk in the light as you are in the light then he has fellowship with you and the blood of Jesus purifies him from his sin. Let _____ recognize that no one is without sin and therefore has no right to get puffed up in his own behavior. Thank you that you promise to forgive the sins of any who confess their sins and agree with you about those sins. Let _____ always know and live his life confessing his sins and being forgiven and to never think that a sin is beyond your ability to forgive. Thank you for being faithful and just as you forgive and purify those who believe in you...

* **WALK WORTHY** *

"Let no corrupting talk come out of your mouths, but only such as is good for building up, as fits the occasion, that it may give grace to those who hear. And do not grieve the Holy Spirit of God, by whom you were sealed for the day of redemption. Let all bitterness and wrath and anger and clamor and slander be put away from you, along with all malice."

EPHESIANS 4:29-31 (ESV)

127

Lord,

Put a guard over _____'s mouth and let no corrupting talk come from it but only that which is good for building up as fits the occasion. You know how discouraging life can be as an athlete when things aren't going as well as they could. Use _____ to be one who speaks in a way that gives grace to those who hear him. Keep ____ from grieving the Holy Spirit by whom he was sealed for the day of redemption. Let all bitterness and wrath and anger and clamor and slander be put away from _____ along with all malice and use him to build up the team and make them stronger without all that junk that tears down. Build _____ into a man of integrity...

"If any of you lacks wisdom, he should ask God, who gives generously to all without finding fault, and it will be given to him. But when he asks, he must believe and not doubt, because he who doubts is like a wave of the sea, blown and tossed by the wind. That man should not think he will receive anything from the Lord; he is a double-minded man, unstable in all he does. "

JAMES 1:5-8

128

Father god,

Thank you that you understand how many decisions _____ has to make every day and how much he needs your wisdom. Thank you for offering wisdom to any who need it and I pray that ____ will recognize his need for you and ask for wisdom regularly so that he can receive it generously from you as you promised to give without reproach. Build ____'s faith so that he prays and believes without doubt. Keep him from being a double minded man who says one thing but believes another. Strengthen his faith to give him a stable foundation for his life. When he does doubt-remind him of Truth from your Word and sustain him in those moments with your presence...

"But he gives us more grace. That is why Scripture says: "God opposes the proud but gives grace to the humble." Submit yourselves, then, to God. Resist the devil, and he will flee from you. Come near to God and he will come near to you. Wash your hands, you sinners, and purify your hearts, you double-minded. Grieve, mourn and wail. Change your laughter to mourning and your joy to gloom. Humble yourselves before the Lord, and he will lift you up."

JAMES 4:6-10

129

Father,

Thank you for grace. For giving grace to the humble even as you oppose the proud. Fill _____ with a humble spirit so that he can glorify you and receive grace. Let _____ submit himself to you so that he can be full of your Spirit and thus resist the devil. Thank you that you offer the strength needed to resist the devil and that it will cause him to flee from _____. Keep the enemy from any role in _____'s life. Help him to cleanse his hands and purify his heart as he continually humbles himself even in this world that seeks to exalt athletes beyond the normal...

* **H U M B L E** *

"Therefore, as God's chosen people, holy and dearly loved, clothe yourselves with compassion, kindness, humility, gentleness and patience. Bear with each other and forgive whatever grievances you may have against one another. Forgive as the Lord forgave you."

COLOSSIANS 3:12-13

130

Dear God,

Thank you that _____ is one of your chosen people, holy and dearly loved, today let him put on compassion, kindness, humility, gentleness and patience because these are all characteristics that come from you and are not natural for man. Help him and his teammates to bear with each other and forgive whatever grievances they might be facing as issues arise from being pushed to the limit on a regular basis. Let _____ remember always to forgive because he has been forgiven and thus have an impact on his team in a positive way that glorifies you...

* FORGIVENESS *

"He has showed you, O man, what is good. And what does the LORD require of you? To act justly and to love mercy and to walk humbly with your God."

MICAH 6:8

131

Father,

With all kinds of opinions swirling around _____ about what he should be doing and what he needs to do, thank you for making it simple. Let _____ understand what you consider most important and thus gain some clarity for his life and decisions. Help _____ place importance on and choose to do justice, to love kindness and mercy and to walk humbly before you God. Make it clear to _____ how he can best make these each a huge part of his life as he continues to become a man of integrity and faith. Give him crystal clear focus in the chaos of life...

* **H U M B L E** *

Made in the USA
Lexington, KY
14 December 2016